Sea Glass Hearts

A Stormy Island Publishing Anthology

ISBN: 9781082422294
Published by Stormy Island Publishing
Copyright © 2019
All rights reserved.

Contents

v

vi

For the children of the sea and the dreamers of dreams.

May you find a drop of hope in these pages.

Poseidon's Domain

Sylvia Riojas Vaughn

Wet, deep, cold, dark,
source of life, myth.
I wade in the surf,
wary of jellyfish
bobbing on the surface
like sandwich bags.
Overhead, gulls laugh,
wings lazily beating.
Golden sunshine spills
over the gentle waves.
Dolphins lead the way
for shrimp trawlers,
splash alongside
catamarans.
Relaxing on the sand,
I contemplate the link
between microscopic
plankton, enormous whales.
How male seahorses
bear the unborn young.
The marvel of an octopus.
In a cloudbank, Pegasus,
admiring his sire's kingdom.

Navigation

Haley Morgan McKinnon

I have heard
that sound travels four times faster through water
than through air, so

if I travel five hours (and 24 minutes)
and end up on the waters of the Bristol Channel
which will become the Celtic Sea
which will become the Atlantic Ocean

if I stand on that pier tonight and
scream your name or
whisper it as if
you were next to me again in the dull rays of morning
as if I could feel your skin on mine instead of
only hear you through the satellites

could that sound find you across all those seas?
do you think it would trip over the swirls of the wind or get stuck
in the narrow channel of the Panama Canal?

would it get distracted
by the bright hints of stars
mirrored on the waves on which it skims,
stars that will pass through

my eyes
                        on the way to
                                                yours?

do you think it could feel how intensely I want you?

do you think it would make it
up the side of Mexico
up the West Coast of the United States
and reach you
before my body ever could?

even though it is deep in dark on this side of the world

do you think the sea could help get my love to you
so it's the first thing you hear
or maybe feel
maybe in a slice of sunlight across your pillow
when you wake on your side?

I'd like to believe that love can cross oceans
even when I
can't

Our Place

Katrina Thornley

We were not the sun and stars,

Or the moon and all the clouds-

We were the fog before the beach—

Mist vanishing at first touch.

Along the Shore

Sara Mosier

he was a beautiful, star-gazer being,
sweat, tears, and sea salt
gilded waves between pages
      which way is right?
      where will
           I
                  find
                        the way out
as my limbs flail and grapple
for a rough surface,
to cling to sea-worn cliffs
      that will only
           make
me
      bleed

Beachside

Jo Barbara Taylor

a simple stone,
burnished like sea glass

confides in the moon
    wanders wide
        tells tales of tides
           and distant shores
    studies stars
        in a mariner's sky
glimpses
        the inexplicable eclipse

wave-washed, it
sleeps in winnowing seagrass

The Angry Sea

Maxine Churchman

The storm-angered sea swelled and puffed its grey bulk against the sky.

Raging and roaring it tore into the beach, grinding and tearing the

shoreline.

Like a ferocious beast it snarled as it dragged the shingle back to its lair

White spume spraying into the wind like spittle from is maw.

Lightening danced across its surface, while thunder clapped in time

And the sea bucked and plummeted as though shaking off their ire.

A Dream of the Sea

Rich Rushell

Isn't there a strange mood in the air
Safe on the shore, curiosity may lead
Walk along wooden boards and out across the sea
Lower ourselves into waters underneath

Let the waters turn
The point of no return
If you're not concerned
There's plenty more to learn

The tide has pulled us out
Our minds are clear of doubt
Can you see through the sand?
Smile and take my hand

Take a look around
Look at what we've found
The sun creates the glare
We're almost out of air

Picking up the pieces of gold and silver off the bed
Precious stones and shells and pearls to decorate ourselves
Time is getting on now as the sun begins to fade
Take a last look around, we must soon be on our way...

The Tragedy of the Wild Heart

Zoey Xolton

Her love was like the sea,

Boundless, ever changing and free.

As beautiful as moonlight on the water,

Of chaos and power, she was the daughter.

Deep, dark and full of secrets without measure,

She guarded her precious heart like buried treasure.

Blue were her thoughts, and blue were her dreams,

She yearned for another's heart to hear her screams.

Unpredictable and strong, her emotions crashed like waves,

Upon the rocky shores of hidden caves.

Perhaps she was looking in all the wrong places?

Judging by wealth, by standing and fair faces.

When had she given up on hope's eternal promise,

Of finding tranquillity, peace and lasting solace?

There was beauty in the wild, in the untamed, the unbroken,

But she'd give up forever to hear those *three little words* spoken.

Agate Beach

Tyson West

i cannot watch
breakers caress the sand – hiss
back but persist
without reliving that dark
night our fingers found their flow

February, 2019

Memories

Quinn Brown

You're gone but
Your music is still in my playlists
In the soaring chords and heartbreak vocals
I see you dancing at 3.a.m

Your makeup is still in my drawer
Foundation that never quite matched your skin
Eyeliner that was always just as crooked
As the stretch marks carved through your thighs

Each dust particle in my room
Carries the scent of your perfume
Sugar and spice and rust and dirt
You were a contradiction

Of Heart, Sea, Salt, and Blood

Persephone Vandegrift

Heart,

today you were speaking of breaking,

and about the time you almost drowned

off the coast of Crete

a thousand years ago.

In that little boat.

Eyes locked on him.

Fingers reaching out

like a Siren trying to take her first soul.

Then over you went

under a mouthful of water

watching the ripples above dismantling a dream.

The salt scratching your breasts.

The blood pounding.

You dropping.

You brought me here, you cried.

I did, I said. I'm sorry. I thought it was love.

Liar, you said, *I don't want to die.*

I know, I said, but you'll have many deaths.

I am sinking, you said.

Seahorses don't, I said.

Your silence as you touched down.

Angry, like a baby.

Beating at me like a storm.

Do you remember I swallowed you

and everything else

just to give you some company.

Even Poseidon was jealous of us that day.

The fisherman still sing of that great rescue

when, before the sun set, I threw you up onto the shore.

You looked just like a starfish.

Arms stretched out for something.

Anything.

I'm still angry, you said. *I will be angry for a thousand more years.*

I know, I said.

Forgive me.

I still have a sea stuck in my throat.

On Assateague Island's Beach

Vonnie Winslow Crist

I do not swim in the ocean—
choosing to bury toes in sand,
allowing ultra-violet rays to crisp my skin,
feeding the legions of gulls,
and gathering scattered exoskeletons.

I do not swim in the ocean—
having felt the tug
when waves lick my ankles,
having felt the need
when a dolphin pod slices the surf.

I do not swim in the ocean—
though my fingers ache
with unseen webbing,
my neck throbs with secret gills,
and hidden scales tingle my skin.

No, I do not swim in the ocean—
because my ears ring
with the songs of whales,
and my salty blood
longs for home.

The Jade Green

Sarah Mahina Calvello

take me to where
the seaweed
meets the water
in a jade green
laugh
and a cry
that crash against each other
at the same time

we're just waves
trying to find our destination
trying to fight against the jagged
and torn
edges of sea foam

I surrender
who I've been
for who I want to be now

just to think
I used to be alive
why did I feel
I had to hide it away
why did I make excuses
of a weak-hearted cry

when I close my eyes
maybe someday I'll understand why
why I set myself aside
from the laughter

now my eyes are too tired
of being weighed down
by the sea
of my own making
pulled away
by the riptide
fingers crazy
and grabbing sand
it's all about which
illusion I chose
I see that now
like a storm you can't predict,
I'm in my chaotic form
watching the sky
darken and lay form
to each rolling wave
colors
of the sunset
reflect like broken glass
on the wet sand

Soft Sand

DS Maolalai

the sea lapped the land
like an animal
drinking. splashed steadily
at night
in shifting whispered
sounds. we drove out there
at 2am
and should have not
ignored the signs
which read such words
as soft sand
and no cars to enter. when we were done
I dropped the condom
out the window,
the cold wind
masking a low splat, and the car
kicked dust
and dug holes
like panicked rabbits. I got out
and tore the sand,
cold like church
stones. 40 minutes
with her
quietly in the car, staring at the city,
as my dignity flew
over my back
with seashells.

The Refusal

Jenny Dunbar

She walked away, turning a heel quietly

pausing a moment to search his eyes.

Enough.

She had reached the dry sand of the ribbon beach pecked clean,

watched it gather on the breeze towards the tide's edge,

she, so very sure, turning on a heel and leaving.

He watched,

bewildered that such absence of conventional exchange held so much

power within its gaze,

and that such momentum had gathered there towards its vanishing point.

A salt gust grazed his cheek and stung, made a tear and tore it out,

wept as he watched her disappear, sultry in long resonance.

Turning, empty hearted, towards the tide wash he cursed his haste and

lamented a hope lost,

the corn- gold moment, gone,

slipped through fingers fickly.

He had always been so very sure.

A Love so Deep

Katherine Brown

I am a woman obsessed
Ocean
Here it is I find rest
Beach
Always want more, never less
Sandy toes
Sounds I love the very best
Rhythmic waves crash

I could sit forever on this shore
Soft white sands
Awed again as always before
Never-ending
It calls to me and I can't ignore
Pounding surf
A raw and magnificent sight for sure
Sun sparkles radiantly

I love to spend hours on end
Beach chair
Soaking up rays, sporting sun-kissed skin
Warm tan
Hours and days easily blend
Time ceases
Restoring my soul, it helps me cleanse
Self-aware

It is no small fling, I can't pretend
Tide rolls in
I am in love with the ocean, I'm all in
Tide grips me

Two Overboard

Johann Van Der Walt

plunged beyond the surf

their bodies dressed in saline rust

and secretly drifted away

only a memory will remain

echoes of former grandeur

an afterthought of an old photograph

they were a sacrifice to the depths

like a dying whale returning

to its rightful place

what other end is more befitting

than dancing in the deep

under the ebb and flow of infinity

When We Met

A. S. Charly

"… for my love…"

Rowling and rumbling,
waves crashing against the shore,
a calming music.

Seawater splashing,
against the ice of my heart,
slowly melting it.

I'm holding your hand,
a radiant blue ocean,
perfect summer day.

Your words are soothing,
washing away my sorrows,
music of the sea.

Moonlight reflecting,
in the sparkling blue sea,
I'd like to kiss you.

The moon and the stars,
none of them compare to you.
You're my brightest light.

Our bodies embraced,
our souls always connected,
everlasting dream.

Like the waves swaying,
we'll dance together through life,
an eternal twirl.

Ever-growing love,
an eternity of joy,
we'll be together.

My love is endless,
stretching afar like the sea,
everlasting love.

The Mermaid

Ashley Lambright

I'm hidden in the sea,
beneath the foamy wave.
My home is in the ocean,
in a dark and mystic cave

I see the sunlight shine,
like glitter all around.
Tranquil and serene,
in the depths that I am bound.

Many a sailor has claimed to see me.
I am sought by all mankind.
I am never really sighted.
I am mystery defined.

Toes in the Sand

Amelia Jane Ronson

I felt you this morning,

> Right before I woke up to an empty bed.

I am warmed by the sun on our sandy shore,

> On our beach.

I long for the time your arms can envelop me with their warmth

> I close my eyes,

> > Cross my hands over my chest,

> > > Clutch my upper arms tightly,

> > > > I can almost feel you.

I listen,

> The tides are rolling toward me,

> > I try to turn nature's song into the sound of your heartbeat
within my mind.

> > > I am momentarily soothed by this life song as it
resonates within my soul.

I taste the salt in the air,

> No, wait,

> > I touch my cheek and realize I am sensing the saltiness
from my tears.

A cool ocean breeze startles me,

I open my eyes,

        Acutely aware of the vast emptiness on all sides of me.

I look up,

      The large cotton clouds pass me by at a quick pace,

        The sky such a bright shade of blue,

          Like your eyes.

I wonder,

      Have any part of those clouds traveled to where you are?

        Have any of the waters rolling over my feet, as I now walk
our sandy shore, come from anywhere close to where you are stationed?

          Could the sweat of your brow have evaporated
and become one with the salty seas?

            Does the salty taste of your sweat as you
endure things, things I can never imagine, remind you of the sea,

              Of our sandy shore?

               Does it remind you of

home?

                    Of me?

I want to tell you about my most significant reminder of you,

      Running my hand over my slowly growing midsection,

        I wonder,

          How does one say such a thing into a receiver,

          Or to a camera lens with a constantly
interrupted signal?

I never dreamed of saying something like this to you from so far away,

Will I be pulling your mind away from your duties?

Am I selfish to tell you, when your primary duty is to stay alive,

To be hypervigilant, alert, and focused?

For our country and for us.

I wish I could tell you on our spot on our sandy shore,

The shore where we first met,

First kissed,

Watched many sunsets,

And a few sunrises.

I fear not seeing your reaction due to bad reception,

I fear that being the last time I see you,

I worry every time could be the last time I see you,

Hear you.

We must be strong,

We will be strong.

I will start by telling you about our day today on the beach,

And I will finish by saying we will be waiting for you to come home to us,

Counting the days,

Until we can all bask in the sun, smell the ocean breeze, and sink our toes in the sand...

My Familiar

Cordelia M. Hanemann

Wake to strange skin
holding you in;
find yourself reading
the body beside you
reaching the body beside you
rearranging the body beside you.

You recognize it,
the contours of a face,
yet, ask, "Whose
spectacles lie curled
on the night table; who
turned off the night light;
whose half-full glass of water?"

Body heat wraps you,
gives a reason to stay
in bed, Sunday morning,
instead of dying.

Silver Helm

Nathan Mosier

I have found
     My own sun
such a marvelous thing that
Brings life but could take it
as well
I no longer desire other-
               worldly things
I will take a castle in the midst of
     Dark, sage pine trees with
 intoxicating pollen and
     A sky that runs to swim in
The Sea
I find my warmth, my happiness
Swords and spears
        Cut close to my skin but
I prevail
     I feel stronger but I often worry I am
              a husk in chainmail

Accompanying the Gull

C. M. Lanning

I watch a gull rise, flying higher on the breeze.
As I sit here in my rubber chair, water near my knees.

The gentle wind moves effortlessly over azure waves.
Much to my surprise, the seagull behaves.

He chooses not to swoop down and attack my food.
For him to steal my sandwich would be awfully rude.

I smell the squishy emerald seaweed washing up beside me.
It clumps up on some weathered driftwood, now unable to flee.

There's an uncommon bond between the bird and I as we share this shore.
We're all alone out here, and the effect is a peace I adore.

A lazy Thursday afternoon shouldn't be spent any other way.
Lying back in my chair, I stretch, and label this a perfect day.

My white and gray feathered friend lets out a mild cry.
"Don't worry," I said. "Nobody is coming to steal your sky."

I close my eyes as a gust of salt air blows over the beach.
The gull decides to climb a little higher, moving further out of reach.

Before me, the Pacific Ocean approaches lazily, drawn by the tide.
Behind me, a national forest folds over the hillside.

I doze off for a bit before awakening to a splash.
Three orcas leap up and then back into the water crash.

The sun sinks low, letting me know the day is nearly done.
Orange, red, and yellow hues paint the sky. It's almost time to run.

Looking around the bay, I notice my feathered friend is gone.
As my toes meet the wet gray sand, I fold my chair, pop my back, and yawn.

My buddy soars over me one more time, letting out a powerful shriek.
"Let's do this again, soon. How about next week?"

Restless Reticence

Shelby Lynn Lanaro

By the bayside, we sat
on a blanket of sassy
lilac. The sun dripped
down the horizon
like spun honey,

and we watched water
pearl on our sand-dusted
feet. Your bare arm
grazed mine – an alabaster
chill in jalapeño heat.

My heart blushed rave
red while any words
we wished we could have
said swept up in ebb tide.

Candyfloss

A. D. Mooney

My fingers found his -
with a fizz, hearts awaken, a frenzy of hiccup beats.

Planted to the ground flowers wrap around
my throat and spew from my lungs;
on my tongue rests a daisy.

Butterfly wings beat me from the inside
and though I try to escape they cling to my stomach
they kick, causing cramps, cracking.

Doves explode beside my ear
blood bursting from bulbous bodies and water hydrants near a
Violent explosion, fallen feathers eroded by acid.

Candyfloss engulfs
my heart and soothes it to
a sticky, dull trudge.

But with pink petal kisses and peppermint sighs
My eyes
drift to a close.

A Tibetan Sand Poem

Ahrend Torrey

~~A Tibetan Sand Poem I Wrote~~

~~—————Next to the Gulf~~

~~Late Last~~

Bliss

Olivia London

Cool waves caress
warm, sandy skin.
Drawing
back,
surging
forward,
tracing paths
with lacy fingers
as time
stands

still.

Anne Bonny Sees a Siren

E.C.M. Rowntree

Ah, you want to hear about the siren. Well,

They say she's dark as no-life
They say she's sharp as salt brine
They say she's lilting soft knife,
She's heartbreak, dashed hope, moonshine,
They say she's sea silk, scalpel,
They say she's bloodrush, plea.
Sailors say
       she's always calling.
       But she never
       called to me.

Yet

       sailing on night's breath
       sword out, fevered,
       sudden, soaked wet
       far from all wisdom,
       deep in the fret
       she
       and
       I
       met.

What was she like? You mean the siren?
She was
Well, she was —
       She was dark as good luck.

She was sweet as salt brine.
She was lilting soft touch,
heart-mend, high hope, moon-mine,
She was sea silk, hair-pull,
She was strong arms, sea.
Sailors,
she was not sing-calling.
Yet sailors, still she
enthralled me.

Winter Crest

Katrina Thornley

The ice surges,
Fighting to freeze,
But weak against
The ripples kiss—
It gives and quakes
Breaks little by little
Until it joins the flow.

Dispatched to a Watery Hereafter

Mark Andrew Heathcote

Soak me with your kisses
Drench me, till I drown,
I no longer want to be rescued
I no longer want an eiderdown pillow alone.

Be a siren in the wind
Let me crash against the rocks
Let the coral reefs of my soul stretch free
Be the kelp that entangles me.

Be the conch shell that calls to my distant heart
Let me fall like an anchor:
Rest like a sunken vessel in the dark
And find only buried treasure.

"Siren, enchanter-
After we've made love
And I'm no longer flotsam,
I'm no longer a cadaver."

Dispatched to a watery hereafter
I'm no longer a Bog Myrtle insect repellent.
Revitalised, I'm a pond-skater dancing on air
Hearing-music violins just-about everywhere.

Soak me with your kisses
Drench me, till I drown,
I no longer want to be rescued
I no longer want to stab, Poseidon's trident
Or take his or any others lion's share or crown.

Sudden Storm

Laurie Kolp

A fleet of thunderous clouds,
color-depleted in their grayness,

approaches from beyond the horizon.
Rough waves lash back

tongue-splashed sassiness
as I slap flat palms on water

then run for cover beneath
a canopy before its final collapse.

My Beloved Son

Gabriella Balcom

Heart of my heart, light of my life,
I so regret that you've endured strife.

Mistakes we have inevitably made
But with time and love, hurt can fade.

Much of who you are—your hopes, dreams—
Lies hidden inside, but honor still gleams.

You are much, much more than my child
And my pride in you is overflowing, not mild.

Courage you have to keep on, to endure.
Strength is not muscles but souls, pure.

I think of you and my eyes light up.
My heart is full to bursting with love.

You never gave up and had hope undefiled.
You're my hero, my precious, precious child

True Love

Melissa Sell

Love doesn't mean a thing
Nothing in this world is true
At least that's how I always felt
Until the day I met you

You were a promise
An answered prayer that the heavens had heard
Even though my lips had never spoke it
My heart knew all the words

My heart is full with you
And I barely remember my life before
I know my time is limited
But there's no one else I'd live it for

You deserve the best
So my best is what I'll do
As I live this life
I live it, my children, just for you

King of my Fire

Nerisha Kemraj

His soul ignites a flame within,
I thought had long died out
Not so very long ago
when my mind was plagued with doubt

The embers burn so brightly now
whenever he is near
Our hopes and dreams are one again
Our love dispels the fear

As long as he is with me,
my fire won't die down
He is my glow, my strength, my fuel
For him, I wear this crown

Fevered Dream

Sara Mosier

The sea is calm
      tonight
through the tides
      their masks
      are hidden
while the roar of the
      ocean fills
         all
      the
cracks between
      my soul
where the emptiness
      lies
      clotted with thickening
cotton
      while the glittering
      of night
mocks me from
      above

The Fisher's Fishy Find

Ndaba Sibanda

warned not to trawl there

he mended his worn nets

and defied and cast them

into that peaceable pool

and caught fish afflicted

with torments and bugs

and fishy bees and wished

the sun would rise and ripen

his tomorrows with insight

that x-rays hidden sorrows

Never-Ending Fourth

Gerri Leen

I stand in front of the old house
Under a dull, still-winter sky
The water a frigid gray
Beach rocks limned with frost

My eyes see cold, but my memories see more

Decades of Fourth of Julys
The house filled with laughter
Guests overflowing outside
Exploring the beach, dipping in toes

People to talk to, places to be alone, both at once

Bright sun makes us seek shade
The whiz-hiss of bottle rockets
Oysters popping open on the fire
I smell black powder all around

My heart races remembering the sound, the fire

Again, a pinwheel escapes its nail
Chases my father down the dock
My nephews grow up
Sparklers give way to firecrackers

My ears ring from the sound; I hear my mom laugh again

Winter night falls around me
Fourth of July still months away

When it comes, I won't be here
It's not our place anymore

But I can see sparks on the water if I look hard enough

Conversations by the Sea

Ximena Escobar

I brought you to the sea,
Edge of ease
Beginning of self,
Tide of verses and mirrors
in my wine glass,

I brought you to see
Look at the horizon,
The smallness of our place
In Time,

See the ancients looking upon us
Below the skyline,
The glow of their melancholy,
Hidden
In the celestial sky of day,

See the explosions
(I dreamt of
Meteors),

Death would come crashing
Like the promise of the waves

But the wave drew back,
I knew it would fall short,
I knew you didn't get it
When I told you,
And you weren't afraid,

But I followed you.

And I cling to your hand
When sea takes me,
to the Space of desolation
Tide brings me back
To the shore of your embrace

You don't follow me,
But you see me.

Nosy

Claire T. Feild

She sits by a window in her two-story
      brick house, contemplating
      all that she sees.

When there are new neighbors, she
      pretends to hibernate inside
      her home, but she nightly leaves
      its quarters to observe the
      movement of every new shapely
      silhouette.

Staring through the holes of her gate
      that still wraparounds her
      home after all the tornadoes
      have clipped her town's
      antiques, she can be nosy
      incognito.

Finally, a new neighbor observes
      her sitting by a window, and
      the woman is not quick enough
      to move her rusty body an inch
      or two.

Two lovers in the pack of the living
      pound their shoulders on her
      front door, but she does not
      answer, a bowl of brussel
      sprouts warm to the touch
      and ready for her to eat.

The lovers, forgetting her, go to the
        woods, where they can kiss
        and finally make love.

One day the woman spots the lovers
        kissing, and she cries because
        she has never come close to
        fondling a man, not even the
        men in her nettlesome dreams.

World

Rich Rushell

Like the fresh, sobering air at dawn,
The golden light of daybreak,
The promise of something new and good;
My thoughts of you when I awake.

Like staring out to sea,
At the endless waves and ocean spray,
An exciting glimpse into the great unknown;
My thoughts of you throughout the day.

Like the comforting rhythm of raindrops,
The sound of distant thunder;
My final thoughts of you
Before I drift away into my slumber.

Fade Away

Ashley Lambright

My body has been broken,
Beaten, bruised and scarred.
Pain is seeping from my wounds,
Emotions have been jarred.
All the walls are caving in,
It's getting hard to move.
The darkness has a grasp on me,
I've nothing left to prove.
Deeper down the rabbit hole,
With every turn and twist.
I cry for help and reach for hands,
Inside the eerie mist.
Sadness overwhelms me,
Fear has all control.
I'm paralyzed, I cannot move,
I'm lost inside this role.
Blinded by your memories,
Drowning in a sea.
Your hands are wrapped around my heart,
Stealing life from me.
I'm begging now, please let me go,
I promise I won't stay.
I'll run and hide, escape this place,
Just let me fade away.

You're a Day at the Beach

CLS Ferguson

The sand scrubs my feet running on the shore
Just allowing the waves to lap the slightest at my toes
Until I'm ready for the plunge
Out I go into the freezing Pacific
Cold, icing the lifeblood in my veins
Riptide threatening to pull me deep, too deep
I let it
Just a little
Then fight and swim my way to gentler water
Rolling as the waves are pulled by the moon
Outshone by the sun in San Diego's July 15th noon
I ride the waves with my body back to shore
The waters hug and caress my curves
Chilling my hips, my thighs, my chest
My arms make their strokes as my legs kick
Lips go blue as the sun sinks beneath the horizon
Mother beckons me back to shore
The car ride home lulls me into a sun-warmed nap
I awaken as we pull into the garage
Manage my way to a hot shower
Discover the places that the sun kissed me too hard
The burns reveal our intimate moments like hickeys in a 19 year old's
back seat
Water pressure removes sand from places I am still discovering on my
body
As I exit the shower, I wrap myself in a soft, dry towel
Take myself to my room
Put on my soft cotton skull-printed pajama bottoms and tank top
As my head rests on my pillow
I still feel the waves

Rolling through my body
Calming and massaging me to sleep
That's what you do to me

Message in a Bottle

Dale Parnell

If you gave me a bottle
Of cold ink-blue glass
I would fill it to the brim
With every memory whispered
Every forgotten lie
And fear and secret
And sealing tight
I would toss it into the ocean
And if the sea is too afraid to remember
Let it wash that bottle back to me.

Music of the Sea

Katherine Brown

I sprint along the deserted beach,
Feeling the sand squish beneath my feet.

I hear the waves crash upon the rocks
And the boats bump against their docks.

Next, I turn my ear to the sky
And listen to the seagulls' cry.

I watch the tide roll in,
Letting the water lap at my shins.

The salty spray hits my face;
I lick my lips and savor the taste.

As the tide goes back out,
Stranded crabs scurry about.

All of the sounds that I hear form the beat
To the wonderful music I find so sweet.

This is where I belong:
Dancing to the ocean's beautiful songs.

The Jellyfish's Tale

Diane Gonzales Bertrand

Conversation stops,
bare feet hop five paces back.

I'm lying on the beach.
Dying.

You only see the blue bloated body,
purple tentacles splayed across evaporating foam.

I'm dying on the beach.

Have you thought of my lonely demise?
You don't offer comfort
or tell my history to your children.
No hymns and eulogy,
or one last drink to my memory.

My funeral is swift—
dig a hole,
scrape my body over
use a mound to cover me up.
Why no sadness as I decompose
under my sandy grave?

With each dig of the shovel, you celebrate
another child's bare foot rescued from my sting.
You smother me, forgotten and shunned
as a nasty creature who must be avoided on all coasts.

No grief, just relief.
Another jellyfish dismissed
from the salty fleet.

What the Water Gave Us

Johann Van Der Walt

how I envy that song
the water whispered
beckoning with steam
as modern currency

ghosts leaked onto the surface
in deafening slices of silence
the night fathomed teen angst
still currents nudge us close

the summer was on your breath
surfing a tide of youth
your mouth was an abyss
 infinite bittersweet motions

the water never whispered again
autumn's curtain call cut the song
now there is a silent theatre
drenched in cushioned sorrow

what was once

can never be again

and what we became

can never be undone

My Greatest Fear

Nathan Mosier

What once had weight,
Matters little now. It is nothing but a,
Grain of sand,
Settled on the endless islands of,
Other memories that once meant more.
Here I sit, castaway amongst these colossal sedimentary mounds,
Some were once like obsidian is to a foreign man.
Something is taken, shaken each time, yet not taken.
At least I hope.
For these grains of sand are what fill my hourglass,
until they all run out.

An Untitled Haiku

Jennifer Carr

Tides of ceaseless sea
rolling through heart's open door
Impermanence

An Ocean Within

Kaustubh Nadkarni

Crisp sand crumbles
with every step.
A footprint etched
for a fleeting moment,
until receding waves
leave a clean slate.
Seashells conceal
the rumbling ocean,
a symphony of sounds,
within delicate spirals.
I stand on the cusp
of sand and water
as the gentle waves
tickle my toes.
My eyes scan
the vast ocean
trying to flood
the chasm within.
The heart yearns,
for entwined hands,
and a pair
of footprints
etched in my soul.

My Heart at Sea

Abigail Wildes

My heart went out upon the sea
Oh, why have you abandoned me

It once was strong and full and bright
But then one day was gone the light

And in its place a sadness dwelled
A sudden darkness left unquelled

As the whole that was my heart
Caught a ship and did depart

'Pon shimmering waves away from shore
To return to me thus nevermore

All of me floats upon the blue
For all of me was held in you

The Visitation

Tyson West

Closing the office early I release my clerk

Into the steady fall of snowflakes

From swabbing the decks into a pretense of anticipation

It was – after all – Christmas Eve.

Besides my current SO needed me

To stop at Sonnenbergs before they closed early

To pick up a pound of sweet – not hot – not hot – Italian sausage

For homemade pizza – her family's Christmas Eve tradition.

The Mario-mustachioed butcher boy

Behind the counter with his Santa hat complimented me

On my defunct title company ball cap

I'd snagged from the garbage at Downriver

After the realtor golf tournament last year

Its bright green on white was enough of a stab at holiday cheer

Among the drab lotto ticket lancers and cigarette scorers for notice.

I was in luck – the mild Italian – not hot – not hot – was on sale

At $1.99 a pound.

I threw the sausage and my hat in the trunk, dropped the mail

Braked barely in time for the homeless couple drizzling

Malt liquor cans and donated scarves

Vagranting across Division in front of traffic in a snow swirl blur

Then drove directly to Deaconess

To a minor miracle bestowed upon me

A meter with thirty-four minutes left.

I had enough nickels from the roll in my trunk

To plug it to a little over an hour.

Then I sauntered into the sterile entry hall humanless

Save for the Filipina janitress who smiled at me

As we wished each other Merry Christmas.

I hit "0" on the grimy push button landline

To get Mary's room number

Walked past ubiquitous hand sanitizers

To enter the tower elevator and pushed its stainless steel button to nine.

The nurse's station displayed cutout cardboard candy canes and one smiling Santa

With a bored bearded nurse in pale blue scrubs

Who pointed out room 912 that Mary shared with Ramona.

Their very own nurse, Linda, massaged her computer, perked a smile

And told me Joan had stopped by an hour ago.

The crisp white sheets of Mary's hospital bed swaddled her

Pale face and hair still mostly natural blonde no makeup

A Welsh death mask in living color.

To my greetings Mary replies

In non-responsive diminished word salad since her stroke three years ago

Linda says she is only getting Tylenol for the pain of her broken leg and hip

She always did have high pain tolerance.

Her hands even as she lay back eyes closed on the pillows

Never stop their fidgeting pull at bandages, wrist bands and catheters

I rat her out to Linda as Mary plucks her IV

Linda velcros a cover over Mary's arm then returns to her screen.

A few minutes later Mary pushes up her oxygen tube nosepiece like a 1960s hippy headband

And I summon Linda again

Who tells me how strong Mary is at 85.

I smile and think you should have felt her body at 45

When we were hot – very hot – at the cabin on Loon Lake

Where we made love all afternoon doors and windows opened

Always with the chance of getting caught as she straddled me

Late in the long summer evenings we thought would never end.

Again I try talking to Mary who mumbles mysteriously

I am not sure she understands or if she even remembers me.

Linda takes Mary's vitals and tells me

How independent and strong-willed Mary remains even in her diminished condition

I smile and tell her I know

The independent ones are the worst patients and, I did not add, the hardest to hold.

Linda grins and adds "except for nurses."

But I told Linda nothing of how well

Mary's lean flesh fit against mine

As our tongues danced pavanes on nerve endings in breast and loin

To leave her austerity crying out the name of a God she did not believe in.

As Santa races around the globe in his sleigh and eight tiny reindeer while

Families begin the opening skirmishes of their holiday together, I have little
to say and

Mary has less to answer – our hands, mouths and genatilia fell silent long
ago

Her strong surreal wrinkle-free features float before me still full of blood –
long wristed hands never resting.

Just before my parking meter expires

I kiss Mary goodbye, then thank Linda –

Only Linda wishes me Merry Christmas.

Mary fidgets her wrist band as I slip into silent night and snow.

In the midst of this wreckage of flesh

I want to scream to the spirits of Christmas past, present and to come that

Love is flesh and the memory of the feeling of flesh upon flesh

Hardwired now into the persistence of my desire for her –

The once and forever love of my life,

But like flesh baby Jesus, those spirits never appear.

As I pass the well-lit plastic crèche in the lobby

I smile at the janitress mopping now

The melting slush from the entryway floor

Then step gingerly onto the sidewalk to my car

Where the steady snow briskly fills my footsteps.

January, 2019

Dying in Color

Robert Beveridge

your love
washes my body
with sharpness

blades
slash
paintings

I lie
crushed
on the floor
below you

lemon
on the tongue

Secrets

Melissa Sell

My life so blue
In the ocean deep
Buried in the sand
Are the secrets
I keep
Rusted ships
Lost now, once missed
Empty embraces, dry lips
Once kissed
Viewing the moonlight
From a depth too dark
Crushed
by heavy waters
And abandoned
by my heart

Some Say the City is Louder

Ahrend Torrey

Some say the city is louder

that it speaks of many, many things.
But I ask:

If you stand in the middle of the city,
what do you hear? The sound of a trolley,
an ambulance, a frustrated driver
behind a braked car?

A bell?   A yell?   A train?

What if you escape—
sail miles and miles, sit under
a blue moon at the edge of midnight—
where waves crash on the shore?

What is louder then, the vast city,
the starry ocean?

What about that silence

                    between the waves?

In My Dreams

Elizabeth Joyce

When I sleep, I dream of you
     and in my dream, the sky is blue.
The ocean's waves caress the shore
     and our feet melt with the ocean floor.
The salty splashes kiss my face
     and you hold me in your sweet embrace.
Your gentle kiss falls upon me
     and we dance our way along the sea.
Our silence tells the love we hold
     and slowly our romance unfolds.
You brush your hand across my cheek
     and I awaken from my sleep.

Atlantis

Haley Morgan McKinnon

you are my Atlantis,
lost in the deep blue of my mind,
buried in the lowest trenches where
no one will ever dare go, or rather
where I will never dare let anyone go

maybe because I am afraid of what they will find, or
maybe because if I let people in
to this city in my mind then
how can I pretend I don't see
the way it's crumbling?

but maybe just for tonight I
can walk with you through the drowned, forsaken streets, and you
can close your eyes

we can lie on our backs
in the soft sand
at the bottom of the sea, and
stare up through the kaleidoscope of blue and green
to the surface, where
our lives wait

and feel the gentle kiss
of water on our skin

we can't breathe but
we don't need to,
as long as I can reach over and find
your hand

and we can stay there forever
in the marvel of the waves

the fish do not care
if we are wrong or right
and the ocean will grow accustomed to the reef
of our naked bodies

as we crystalize
as we stay

The Dahomian

Amy O'Shaughnessy

For my grandfather, Captain John (Jack) Raeburn, and all those on-board the Dahomian on the 1st April, 1944.

Drop to the deep
past the blue
through plankton bloom
fathoms and fathoms down
dark water thickens cold
chill weight crushes
all air out.
Look to the light
bubbles race beyond reach
beyond breath
but there's life here
dusky shark, dog fish, box jelly.
Amongst it all
the *Dahomian* slumbers
under sand sheets
lulled by the Benguela current
adorned with sun-burst coral
dripping with rusticles.
She remembers home
Liverpool
dockers hauling, sweating, swearing
consuming cargo until
belly weighed low
she churns Atlantic seas
headed south.
The *Dahomian* dreams
explosions, shudders, shouts
"Abandon ship!"

a change of course
down, down, down
to this final port
where creatures busy
in her ironwork
cape congers thread through
the jagged breach
eagle rays dust decks
while deep in her hull
a consignment of planes
rusts, forever grounded
roses, primrose, forget-me-nots bloom
on Dora's wedding china.

How it is with You

CLS Ferguson

Something about the bite of the evening air
mixed with the sharp smell of pine
I am 16 or 17 again
There's a sick in the pit of my stomach
20 years ago this was due to a deep insecurity and fear of the future
Now it's just an aching and longing for you
You have renewed my youth
reignited my passions

We didn't dress up our baggage
and set in a corner
in hopes that it would remain undiscovered

Instead we brought it to the center of the room
opened it up
showed each other each item that had brought us
shame
pain
worry

No rejection
Only hope
Love

My heartbeat has changed
My heart beats within you
And yours within me

Indecision

Jeanette Loretta

Indecision reigns like a ruler in between us
Let's break it in two, half for me, half for you

And lay down our intentions to measure their worth
Calculating baggage, estimating damage

If hunger overcomes us
And deprivation defends treason
If rapture disrobes prudence
And risk eclipses reason

If our halves reach whole
And desire trumps demands
Let's put away our tools
And start working with our hands.

True Love

Gerri Leen

Love isn't cotton-candy romance on a beach
Walking hand in hand as the sun goes down
Or running headlong through a field, hair streaming
Twirling as you finally meet in the middle
Your laughter filling the air

Love is black moments when all seems lost
Knowing the one you want is far away
Holding the thought of them as tightly as you can
To keep you safe even though they're gone
The night will end

Love is moments called from time, shared memories
Laughing at the silliness you've lived
Sighing at the hurts you've inflicted on each other
All for the sake of passion, when letting go might
Have been easier

Love is the stillness of a darkened room
Hands entwined, whispered sorries echoing
As you beg forgiveness for what you've done
Your bodies pardon each other long before
Your hearts catch up

Love is a silent moment in an empty room
Trying to ignore the words that ring into infinity
They're gone, they're gone, they're gone
Knowing that for the time you had, you loved
If nothing else, you loved

Beautiful Creature

Ashley Lambright

The sun is shining in my eyes
Glinting off the water's rise
I see a form emerging now
It isn't human, anyhow

The beautiful creature from the sea
Crosses the sand and approaches me
Eyes dark as night, hair like the sun
Hands to hold, legs to run

It smiles at me and beckons behind
I'm suddenly rising, I've lost my mind
I follow him helplessly into the sea
I am not worried, I will be free

The Sea, The Song

Jo Barbara Taylor

Boat, tiny on the horizon,
dances on white caps
like a featherbed fluffed in the air.

Attentive to swells and dips,
a mandolin in the rain singing
a song about someone
I've known a long time.

Lore in *la mer* and the chantey
of longtime, far flung love.

The Hurricane

Laurie Kolp

when I crawled through water
I crawled through water weightless

every effort spent on resistance
was spent anchoring my knees to clay

before erosion swept away the night,
swept away and washed away all thoughts

afforded on my own: words I wished
to say to you, whispers drifting through

my subconscious, weaving through your eye
a flood of tears

I'm Okay

Nathan Mosier

Hot showers that last forever,
because there is never somebody next to you.
Possessions replace people.
They litter your shelves like the dust they collect,
because they cannot hurt you or leave you.
Sleep is rare,
because you can only hold your pillow to,
pretend nothing has changed.
There must always be music, something to do,
because the sound of silence is,
loud enough to numb the ears.
Like bitter winds in late December.
But at the end of the day,
what's on the inside doesn't matter.

I'll just say I'm okay.

Mermaid

Mark Mackey

Like countless times in the past
She saw him through
the miles of brilliant salty sea
Acting like a barricade
between them
She, a being forever destined
to call the ocean home
He a mortal air breather
Who could not
She opted to dispatch
her forever undersea
citizenship
Become mortal
Her tail helping
propel her
Up toward his
vessel
She'd soon have her heart's desire
He stood staring down at her
She yearned desperately for him
Soon they'd be together in undying
companionship
Her tail fell away
Replaced with mortal legs
She broke through the sea's surface
'Come to me beautiful sea mermaid
Be mine forever'
He called out to her
She smiled, achieving her dream

A Crash in the Night

Sara Mosier

an ebony wingspan
ruffles feathers
        that
stretch out across
countless nations.
     His dark hair,
         falling
across his furrowed brow
          like
a veil
    while weak and whispered
truths swim
       in
          a
vast sea of
       violet
         stars
his all-knowing
    gaze
painting the valleys
    and souls
    below
while he draws shadows up
beckoning them
    from
       the
         earth
faithful followers
       rising

                              while
he takes flight
              through the
grey,
              gauzy,
                        clouds

Hyderabad Calling

Johann Van Der Walt

in the lobby
along concrete infinity
your rampant scent
hovers like a drone

an enthralling trail
of phantom lure
calling out fiercely
reaching even my cavities

the fluidity
of this moment
as I near the door
burns like embers

I flood your apartment
like an assiduous wave
an answer to a mesmeric storm
for which we suffer embrace

all of it:
vivid, silky
sticky and
sweet

sumptuously engrossed
in supernova
where we are
finally complete

Diaspora

Leela Soma

One book closed, another opens, a new leaf each day
a dangerous crossing on the Mediterranean Sea,
experiences new, strange sea, enervating
new language, sounds, melodies, tastes to savour
slowly settling to a new rhythm, adapting to change.
The memories flash in the inward eye, shadows never
forgotten, picking an old book, thoughts like a flowing river
invisible, shimmering in the starry nights, dream scenes
On the sea, waves beating like silent drums, turning old pages
Dog-eared, much loved, scented, wrapped with emotion.

Wave of Regret

Ximena Escobar

Sink your absence in a sea of forgetfulness,

Sink my hurt of your silence,

Sink the scream of my frustration

Breaking,

With relentless coldness

(Of blade, Of salt)

(In wound),

Sink my humiliation

Of loving you

Still,

In the nauseating restlessness

Of losing you.

Herring Cove

William Doreski

Fog upholsters Herring Cove,
snuffing the sea horizon
with Leonardo's *sfumato,*
obscuring distinctions you
and I used to think mattered.
Surf has rounded the beach stones
so they gloss in the fitful rain.
Slickered up for the weather,
we pose in various poses
safely distant from each other
to maintain the *you* and *I.*
A few islets drift through the mist,
then nothing but raw Atlantic.

We could walk to Iceland from here
on Campobello, where tourists
in brighter weather play golf
and spend US and Canadian
dollars with equal fervor.
We could walk if the water
were only the ghost of water,
as it seems to be at this moment.
But to punctuate the absence
of form, a seal head perks
from the gray, a black rubber nub
smirking as it confronts us.

Lending weight to the filmy air,
the seal head nails us to a view
we had hardly thought a view

a moment ago. We shuffle
closer to each other and stare
so hard at the water that one
more seal head appears. Two
look at two. Now the sea, lacking
the imperative of surf, closes
gently over the slick black spots
to leave us staring more deeply
into nothing we hadn't noticed
was nothing two minutes ago.

The Beach

Lisa Van Der Wielen

The warmth of the sun,
The soft white sand.
The salt in your hair,
Sun kissed and tanned.
The ripples of water,
As waves crash to the shore.
Then pull away again,
For another encore.
The rhythm of the ocean,
The musical notes.
Of sand and water,
Shells and sailboats.
Aqua blue colours,
The smell of sea air.
The calming of the beach
Helps the soul to repair.

Sinner

Quinn Brown

You know, lust is one of the seven deadly sins

The Devil chuckles as you push her against the wall, intertwining your slender fingers with her calloused ones. Her hands are stained with crimson ash, and her eyes flicker with the same fire that you feel in your chest when you look at her, as if she knows how desire has charred your bones. When you kiss her, she tastes like wood smoke, and her tongue is coated with the filthy secrets of a thousand damned souls. Each of your curves melt into hers until you can't tell where her deviance ends and your righteousness begins. With her head between your thighs, blasphemy falls from your ambrosia-stained lips, things so foul it makes even her blush the colour of hellfire. Her fingers slide underneath your skin, winding through your ribcage and claiming your heart as hers. As if you ever had a chance to defend it. As if it wasn't hers already.

You're worth sinning for

The Universe

E. M. Eastick

The universe is waiting, it's dark within my soul;
It's pushing to escape this world and let the stars unfold;
It flickers and it flashes, a light within the dark,
Searing through the skin of me and pulling at my heart.

The world is but a tiny thing compressed within my mind,
Expanding through the narrow thoughts and spinning all the time,
Providing music for the dance and gardens for the stroll;
Protecting all the darkness of the universe—my soul.

The pain cannot be buried, the fear cannot be guised,
When one persists in seeing things through crystal-coloured eyes.
Resistance is a must, or else the fire chars,
But never had I counted on your galaxy of stars.

The whirlwind of your decency, the roaring of the sea;
The mystery within the swirl of blue serenity.
The questions and the answers, in silence and in words,
Pursuing me down misty straights and round forbidden curves.

A day of exploration; a lesson set in space;
The miracle of slow release, a concept to embrace.
To listen is to board the ship that takes me to the moon;
To orbit is to enter space that I will cherish soon.

The universe is endless; infinity is there,
Forever floating deep inside on dark, forgotten air.
It lies in hidden coves, it longs to live in you.
It opens to the only one my universe could know.

The storm of you comes rumbling, the light is harsh and kind,
A lightning bolt of honesty, so difficult to find.
A shock of timeless power, to break down ancient doors,
The universe is open now; this universe is yours.

Ocean's Dancers

Katrina Thornley

The seaweed sways,

Couples dancing

Forever in time with waves-

The ocean's peaceful captives.

A Christmas Tree, Galleon

Mark Andrew Heathcote

Galleon lit up like a Christmas tree
Anchor rose, sailing out of port to sea
It looks for the world like a many-tiered
Wedding cake, but no bride is perceived
Guess her handsome groom has her below deck
Coiled around him like some clinging whelk
Yes the whole scene's out of a fairy tale
At this moment she's ready to unveil
Let this maiden voyage truly begin
A toast to their future shipmates with gin
And sail this 110 guns galleon to the moon
Salute these newlyweds on their honeymoon.

A Dance with the Sea

Sylvia Riojas Vaughn

Swells surge to shore,
mighty blue curls topped with froth.
Originating in the vast expanse,
driven by ferocious storm gales,
they crash onto sugar white sands.
A surfer tops a crest,
baggies sticking to skin.
Crouched on the board,
arms stretched out,
one skyward, one grazing an ankle.
Right foot, in a ballet arabesque.
The ocean, an unpredictable partner.
Golden sunlight bathes the dark form,
clouds mount menacingly offshore.
My camera captures the fleeting moment.

Her Eyes

Robert Beveridge

flecked sapphires
faultless washed
clear by rain

Love Me

Sioban Timmer

Love me like the sea
With crashing waves and lapping tides
In ripples that radiate over the expanse of my being

Love me like the sky
From horizon line to breadth of blue
In shades too countless to be perceived by the soul

Love me like the moon
When rounded full with circling halos
In hues of perfect silver that melts two silhouettes to one

For that is how I love you
As though the sea, and the sky, and the moon
Exist only for reflection

Granted

Nathan Mosier

waking each forecasted morning
not bothering to climb stairs
to kiss her goodbye
eating the same drink
awake, yet
                  still dreaming
zombified over too many words
             read
hateful eyes and stronger guys
burning mental waste with a run
and weights
my drug is tighter skin
for I seem to have nothing else
cycling by the lake can be
                      the same
asleep one moment,
                awake again
nothing worth
            remembering
and maybe that's just how I like it...

Popping Candy

A. D. Mooney

My mind clouds over

sticky steam clings to eyelashes

Pulses

drag

Fingertips make dents, dizzy

static cracks at the back of a delicate spine

lips curl upward

sizzling with suggestion

breathing quickens

candy pops

Back Arches

Precious Seconds

Joanne Alfano

you turned away
and in a few precious seconds
it was over

i turned the other way
collected my thoughts
headed for a future

if my life is now seconds,
it is precious seconds
that fill me

Fisher's End

Maxine Churchman

He spurns the comforting warmth of bed
Rheumy eyes peer through dirty panes
At frenzied activity below his croft
As boats are readied in Blackrock Bay.
His gnarly hands pluck restlessly
As fishers make their haste to leave.
Coloured hulls churn brackish water
Racing 'cross the grey-green sea.
His gloom is for a life becalmed
To miss the spray and open sky
Exhilaration, joy and pride
To haul aboard those slipp'ry lives.
It's hard to fathom tougher efforts
Long hours, sometimes days at sea
Risking life and limb each outing
For a catch that we may eat.
"A well-earned rest," his son describes it,
Unwitting source of his despair
To end his days marooned, unwanted
Sinking slowly from inertia.

Noise below and rapid footsteps.
"Gramps Gramps a boat is ours.
Today Bill Fry will take us out
I want to fish, please show me how."

Pearls

Olivia London

Words spoken in the dark
Find their way easily
Into my heart.
They fall into my ears
Softly
Like grains of sand.
I hold them close,
Shape them.
Polish them until they shine.
I collect them one by one
Until they wrap gently around my neck
Where they all sparkle and dazzle for a while.
In the silence, time passes.
They become dull, faded,
Until they choke the air right out of me.
A violent storm churns
So deep within me
I fear I'll never escape.

Poem

Jenny Dunbar

She walked, eyes transparent as the Shetland sea,

thought of the mirror glass, its sullen bloom obscuring the image,

high across the sound gulls trawled, reeling in polyphony, breaching the shoreline,

long ago in a small acre she stood with her man, was with her man,

the words ran in her mind carrying her back to black earth across flat lands

the bark of a dawn fox at the furrow's edge.

Sea-Spun

Sara Mosier

They rise up from a bruised
      sunset,
aching,
   lonely.
the cotton nature of their
     caress
            grazes the surface
of
    the
          sea
like the most subtle and
faintest brush of
         too soft lips,
ever careful,
     ever mindful
        of their brief
encounter that is rare and smelling of
         earth.
Palm to palm
     in a fog sodden veil
hidden away from the world
while the waves break apart
     every bit of truth
          every
secret spoken, hushed between them
as they close their eyes
     with the sun sinking
into the horizon
       destroying
another day

Fishing for the Words to Say 'I Love You'

Shawn Klimek

To say "I love you" is less than true,
By which I mean to say,
The truth is that I love you more
Than three mere words convey.
The phrase flits like a silver fish
Within a sea of grey,
Which can imply a school of fish,
Yet not all fish portray.
A metaphorical fisherman,
With nets behind his craft
Might catch the words I'm fishing for,
Still missing from this draft,
And sell them to a sushi chef,
Of literary bent,
Who'd clean and prep them with such love,
You'd know just what it meant.
But wait. Although this poem falls short
——it rambles on and such,
Just measure how it fails and know:
I love you twice that much.

Masterpiece

Ariella Vasquez

You brush against me.
I burst with effervescent hues of bliss.
The sky is stained with a permanent glow,
our splattered souls on display.

Dazzling streams of consciousness
cascade down like ribbons from a gift.
Magnetic memories coat the walls of our minds.
What a beautiful mess we've made.

I See the School Board

Ahrend Torrey

I see the School Board
    Rush into the Cafe

They're stunning
    in their black and
        white suits, like terns

off the shore of Aruba, soaring
    in to work, typing a bit,
       drinking a glass

of lemon water only.
    They clap
       their computers

after 10 minutes:
    push them
       into their bags, flee

the table, leave only a feather
    of paper. Once here,
       now gone, they soar—

into the world—
    making it beautiful!
    — I'm hopeful—
    and more beautiful!

Wind at Headland

Naida Mujkic

I was slowly climbing up

The steep stairs

I left behind the sea

Mermaids on the rocks that

Were making chamomile wreaths

But I didn't turn around, until

The wind whirled my scarf

And lifted it high above

It seemed to me that it drifted it

To the lighthouse keeper who was standing

In front of the lighthouse

This is when we met: I was being silent

While the sea was being adorned with chamomile

Because it had nobody else

And when I got back to my road again

The lighthouse keeper was no longer

Greeting me

The cold wind gave me shivers

It hurried all the way from the South Pole

My scarf was its mound

With a half-smile, as the courtesans
do

Re•sil•ience n.

Diane Gonzales Bertrand

Port Aransas, Texas after another hurricane:
cars line up in funeral procession as island residents
return to assess and rebuild in the same sentence.
Plywood eye patches swollen over the windows and doors
from whipping winds, blankets of water.
Neighbors return boats parked in the wrong front yard,
the mayor delivers bottled water from his golf cart.
Fishermen carry mop poles, shovels, and brooms
to help clean up the only grocery store on the island.
Summer home refugees stumble past wood frames with no roofs,
metal buildings gnarled like rheumatoid fingers.
Souvenir stores with vacant windows stare in open disbelief.
One old welder pats the upright steel beam of a carport
he built with his brothers, sons, and grandsons,
walking distance from the empty channel
where once a pier stood across churning waters.
Islanders whistle against another storm,
another year, another decade.
Accept curfew, mosquitos,
shortages on batteries and clean water.
Port A locals dry off, share a beer,
revive their salty stubborn ways.

Titillation

KB Baltz

On the cold dark days

of midwinter

murmurations of starlings

flit upon thick limbed oaks

to burrow inside her hollow places

huddled together

languid in each other's warmth.

Branches bend under the weight

of appreciation

and the sighs of feathers

leave winter's bite electric.

They fly as one,

leaving earth and tree

shaking

naked

alone

touched by ten thousand feathered breasts.

Yellow Moon

Mark Andrew Heathcote

I want to get intoxicated
I want to sit beneath a yellow moon
And drink red wine while we dine
Looking deep into each other's eyes

I want to drown and get woozy...
When the jazz of what we both do
Makes me tipsy,
Makes me lightheaded

I want to get intoxicated by you
I want to sit beneath a yellow moon
And row my arms out to you
For shore leave,

Love, what do you say
Can you be a tropical island?
With a Hawaiian sway
Can I write my SOS on your soul?

Will your heart be the raft that saves me?
Oh, I want to sit beneath a yellow moon
And fall fathomless under your spell
Oh, I want my heart to levitate

I want my body to fall down a well
And find its walls contain all of me!
And find I'm inside of you
And you're like a yellow, intoxicating moon.

Second Chance

Sheila Verano

You came to me like a fast-moving wave
Shook my world then left me hanging
Until now I can remember how it happened
My heart that you stole just like a thief.

But then you come back when the sun rises from the horizon
Mend this broken heart of mine
And show me that second chances are worth it
And love wins no matter what choices it makes.

Blue

E.C.M. Rowntree

Race down the sand the waves chase up
breath ragged t-shirt flapping –
a t-shirt, in this weather –
smell the old salt
and the fresh tide
and the seaweed laid out like mosaics
smeared in sand;
sky's blue
sea's blue
you're jagged hopeless tearaway blue,
tear-your-heart blue, tearing up blue –
but reach the water

gasp

and it kisses the skin between your naked toes
and it says nothing to you.
It swirls. It's cold.
Sand moves. Tide rolls.
You go deeper.
Wind tugs at your ratty old shirt
a t-shirt, in this weather
with holes.
Chest soothes. Blood scalds.
You go deeper.
Turn and look at the bay, see figures, far away;
raise your hands, blue hands –
perhaps if they've seen you
they think you're drowning.

Sea tugs, pushes
says nothing to you and isn't about you
blue, cracked blue, old and deep-down blue
and you are not drowning.
You are raising your hands
you are only waving,
blue-waving
to the figures on the far-off shore.

Against the Grain of History

William Doreski

From the window of the bedroom
in which Eleanor Roosevelt
bore her first child, the fog-
struck bay looks too opaque
to allow a small boat to pass.

The tour guide's dramatic spiel
washes over me, eroding
my sense of the past. Ghosts
fled this cottage years ago,
leaving it to governments
to divvy like Christmas dinner.

The fog looks alert, touchy
as flesh. If it comes ashore
with its tough, granular half-tones
it could lick flesh from bone
the way all real carnivores do.

In clear weather a strong swimmer
could splash from here to Eastport,
trailing a prismatic glitter.
But in this fog that swimmer
would paddle in circles before
sinking to the silt with regrets.

I want to linger in this bedroom,
sit on the bed and watch the fog
thin until the vague outline
of the other shore appears,

encrusted with wooden houses.

Although the tour shrugs along,
dragging me against the grain
of history, I hear the bay
lap at the shore, drinking
deeply from the atmosphere,
consuming everything in gray.

Solo Flight

Katrina Thornley

"It is nature"

He says,

"For the birds to depart"

And I wonder,

What of the lonely goose,

In the half-frozen pond

Who paces patiently,

With a knowledge

Even he can't understand.

A Twist of Gears

Nathan Mosier

Melodramatic realities
                 Infest comforts
like taking hot baths on
           Cold days
People with fox ears
Hear the ticking of
                    wrist watches in an
empty space
everything is important
                 one moment
and is worth nothing
                 the next
Everything is Nothing and Something
                        all at the same time
           Time
Ticktock
           Ticking
                 Tocking
                      Helplessly
Nothing to stop what comes
                 Tomorrow
There will be no such thing as
        the Day before
                 Yesterday
there is only what is now.
and Now has already past.

Remembrance with You

Ximena Escobar

Your chest is all I think of
When I think surrender,

On sand, they fell
Like sunshine
To rest.

I land on you
Sink in you
Burn on you

Salt of the earth,
Is you.

Making the Most of It

DS Maolalai

that's what's best;
sleeping til noon
on our last saturday,
with the air burned orange through the curtains,
outside
staved off
like thunder
and a rabbit at the mouth of a burrow.
in the playa
dogs
tear the legs
off dead birds
and the waves which strike the seaside
with a sound
like newspapers being torn
forever. it's the last day
of the holiday
and you roll over
and prop yourself up, wedging an elbow
in your sandy
bathing suit,
suggesting we get up,
get dressed
and make the most of it. I pretend
not to hear you,
melting myself in the sheets,
making the most of it.
making the most of it.
making the most of it.

Salty Ocean Waves

Ashley Lambright

The salty ocean waves
Licking at my toes
Warm me to the soul
And wash away my woes

There's healing in the water
You only have to ask
Give away your troubles
Let the ocean do its task

I see the moonlight glinting
On a foamy, rolling wave
I wade into the waters
Feeling less than brave

My sorrows fade away
As I swim into the deep
Tranquil and serene
I begin to drift to sleep

Peacefulness replaces
The pain I felt before
I drift into oblivion
As my body floats to shore

The salty ocean waves
Greet me like a friend
The moonlight shines above me
This is not the end

Moonlight Kiss

Cordelia M. Hanemann

Clouds court the night sky;
long bone of white moonfall tracks
the black lake: shining arms creep
along the shore, confine water's dark core.

Deep hungers rumble, and the trotline stirs:
your thumb curls round the barb as you grip
the quivering body, strip the catfish skin
with blunt-nosed pliers; I break open the bread's crust.

Repast: our mouths close on crisp flesh,
hot from the grill. Wanting the kiss, I enter
the room of your mouth. Tablet of fire, acid
eating our tongues; we didn't know we'd lose our faces.

Skin, legs, curl of bodies: hot breath
of summer air molten core at Earth's heart.
Volcanoes know nothing of this fire:
tearing our skins each from each.

Fate

Nerisha Kemraj

History repeats itself
in the blink of an eye
Lovers find love
And are destined to die

They find one another -
soulmates for life
United again
In their afterlife

Try as one might
to break them apart
They'll win the fight
for even in Death,
they cannot part

Moses Lake

Tyson West

I could describe its geology
Great glacial scratches in the dark moon of the basalt basin
With arms like a funnel web spider
Nesting below the Grand Coulee
Drain and depository for all the moisture in this sagebrush sea.
Or I could sing the double fugue of sun and moon blazing in counter point
Drying the grass and cooling the night
To perform the miracle of raising dust and straw in micro tornadoes as
Its namesake parted the Red Sea.
As I ride I-90 westward the fresh greening
Circles and square signs phosphorescent against parched bunchgrass sing out
Wagnerian roads named for German pioneers
Whose heirs in cowboy hats drink whisky not schnapps and cling to their
dry homesteads with Teutonic furor.
NPR from Spokane fades and
Statics into the Español and mariachis of the Quincy station
So I can brush up on high school Spanish to the accompaniment of Flaco
Jimenez.
At least Germans and Mexicans all agree on accordions.
I pass through the bubble of feed lot flavored air before I skirt
The arsenic green golf course belt along the shore where the roadway
crosses
An arm of the lake – a relic of ice age floods.
Moses Lake was at once all these things to me and nothing more
Until you told me
How your father flew his desk at the air base there
Pack of bare-ass Camels in his blue pocket
Dispatching silver jets to boom across the cerulean cold war sky

While you and your sisters had risen before him
To water ski the desert lake's alkaline waves
Riding over the ramp to hone your form and figures
Proving women as well as men can compete
Over and in absolutely anything.
I could not help feeling a slash of concern as you told me
How you gashed your leg and your twin took you to the ER for stitches
Calling your dad
He stayed at the base to helicopter there
After all you were still walking and talking.
You three took first place that weekend
Even with your bandaged leg.
No matter how many glistening plastic boxes
For fast food may blossom on Highway 17
North towards Ephrata or south towards Othello
No matter how green the East Low Canal may pull water from Roosevelt
To spin the aluminum circles that paint greater balls and boxes of ground
in cadmium green
This place is forever frozen in 1964 to me
Long before I came here
As glaciers and great floods once worked their magic
Your past is always and forever
My present abraded into me from the pain and the pleasure in your touch.

November, 2016

Silence

Leela Soma

The unsaid words hang in my throat
lips bitten red raw, the bitterness
swallowed with rising bile, as the sea moaned
and waves crashed against the grey rocks
silvered by the crescent moon, hanging low
we sat in silence, lay on the cool sand.
Hours later we watched the horizon brighten,
sky turned pale pink to gold streaking the blue
gossamer clouds floated, transient as our rows
drifted away, the pain inside subsided like
the white froth of the waves lashed on the
rocks and gently returned to the blue sea.

Distance

Jenny Dunbar

'On a clear day you can see across,' she said
'The outline of rock and sea edge, sand and dune,
the side of the tide's hours, a touch away,
a hand's grasp.

'On a clear day, once, a full tide rolled swollen to the brink and churning,
further out and burning, distressed cargoes floundered,
in the instant of dawn light the sight lines dimmed, obscuring the
whisper of
touch and reach,
no causeway beckoned along the swept dunes' rim,
only the obsolescent icons of wood drift and steel,
rusted fragments in the bird morning, a hand's grasp away,
a touch too far.'

An Incestuous Tango

Claire T. Feild

Jocasta stares at Oedipus with a query
as his looks reflect hers, his show of
enigma, the encouragement she needs
to place him in thralldom to her ways.

Her vulturine eyes scare him at first,
but the loveliness of her body is his
only thought. How he can possess
her he will leave to Jocasta.

She acts quickly, squirming before
his eyes, no illusion, his usual
bombastic voice transformed to an
aphonia by her presence.

She leans toward him to hear his
whispers of love, the tango of feeling
between them resulting in a kiss
so formal that she wonders if her
ploys will ever work on a man
who, unlike her, is no veteran in
lovemaking as he is in war.

Yet she succeeds in seducing him
to marry her, the plan to change
him into her lover working because
he really does love, even if he
will have to leave her soon to
go back to fight a war he hates.

Tasting the Sea

Olivia London

Like the first lingering touch
of a lover's hand,
sweeping over your back,
their warm breath
kissing the soft skin
of your neck as you wake.
The first brush of their lips
against your own,
exploring, discovering, insistently questioning,
until you can't breathe…

but you don't need to.

You breathe through the taste of their lips,
their salty breath.
You live solely on the sound of your heart

beating

beating

beating

in time with the waves.

Beyond

Malina Douglas

The ferry hums,
sways slightly as it moves

I wander through carpeted lounges lit,
push open heavy double doors,
step onto the deck:
brisk wind, the wide sea flat
and steel-grey from woollen clouds
clustering like knitted brows,
frowning.
The green and softly rounded hilltops
grow smaller as we drift.

Again to the deck—
green land is gone
and clouds have blown away
revealing sky,
sun shines, and the sea
is a shimmering sheet of silver
as if hammered by a smith.

No land in sight,
yet far beyond the horizon's line
in a land of green pastures,
a curving river,
and tidal mud flats
strewn
with abandoned boats,
my love waits.

The ferry hums,
sways slightly as it moves
and I stand at the ships rail gazing
as every rumbling moment brings me closer—

my love waits.

Oceanic Adoption

Johann Van Der Walt

urged on by the first light

the mild shallows

suddenly reveal a clear-grey tide

thousands of swells ripple gently

casting hills of glass crusted golden sand

filling the grooves underneath my feet

unruffled waves serenade the gulls

in meticulously well-timed sun fractures

that etches across the moving swell

it's all intricately connected

bound to the tremulous ebb and flow,

gradually the ocean even appeals to my bones

on land I have fallen and lost my way

but these tides know only about sweet embrace,

and disregard all resistance into the murk

water sand currents waves salt
I dissolve within this living structure
there is no human or fish or sea

I emerge and inhale deeply,
undoubtedly forever part of the ocean,
her water now runs through me

Endurance

Sarah Mahina Calvello

there's an
unexpected art
in endurance
grasping onto
what I
think reality
is supposed
to look like

memories never
leave your bones
bad and good
traces skin
edges of stars
play in dreams

a calming sound
a sea salt kiss
everything
lain out
like a map
of the heart
never to be
pulled apart

I'm a book
leaf through
my pages
take the time
to actually know

Noctis Mare

Robert Beveridge

for Allison Thomas
"There is no power/so great as love/which is a sea..." --WC Williams, "Asphodel, that Greeny
Flower"

the feel of your tongue
against my wrist;
the liquid inward gasp,
green beneath the dark.

I kiss you in night air,
salt and lust for fire,
for liquid,
the first rays of light
to stroke your legs, your hips,
the taste of you,
salty moisture beaded still
against the tang of flesh

Abyss

Ariella Vasquez

Lost souls drifting at sea.
Aggressively guided
Through tumultuous waves of uncertainty.
Saltwater drowns their hopeless lungs.
Dreams crushed. Reality sinks in.
The silence is deafening.

Distance

Jeanette Loretta

Distance is a kind of death
Its magnitude, an ocean's breadth
Profoundly, an abysmal depth

Impervious to sentiment
It conquers every argument
and shrugs at the predicament

Stretching hearts, reckoning souls
Distance endures, separation grows
Hope pulled thin concedes its holes

There's only one sure remedy
to cure the ambiguity
and distance is the enemy.

The Sea is Many Different Colors

Haley Morgan McKinnon

at the line
where the dark shadow of the storm clouds meets
the bright green of the unsuspecting sea –
that's where I left you

in 100 years when the ghost of the woman who loved you
walks along the edge of those waters,
will I find you in the sand?

will you survive the assault of the ocean's indifference?
for you
are nothing to her
but an empty shell
of a man
broken open by the salted fists,
dispersed by the incessant pull
apart of your wearied bones

can you withstand
the total breaking
of your heart
by not one woman,
but two?

and when I find you again,
will I recognize your pieces

among the rest?

The Sea's Embrace

Maxine Churchman

What chance had I against such angry adoration?
She held his changing moods, at once dark and violent;
Then soothing as a lover's breath upon her soul,
And wrapped them about her like a cloak against the world.

Impotently I watched, as she stood upon the shore
Hour upon hour, day after day, for all the time after.
He'd kiss her feet and she'd go to him, ever deeper
Giving in to his embrace, so empty and cold.

I tried, I really did, but I wasn't what she needed.
I saved her time after time. Waiting... loving ... hoping.
But the call to her was always too strong to resist,
And she would return, to drown her constant demons.

Each day she'd grown more distant and I'd despaired
Until she slipped away, unseen, to be with him forever.
When finally I saw her floating there, peaceful and serene
I beat my chest in fury, for I'd lost her to the sea.

Violet Returns

Ximena Escobar

She didn't understand his coldness.

She didn't understand his restless murmur of here

and away.

She didn't understand the cloud of his heart,

Buried secrets she felt in her own bones.

Cells stirring,

Waiting.

She longed for his depth.

Overwhelming reflection of the sky.

Her smallness longed to disappear

In the immensity

of his wisdom.

He pushed her away,

He warned her with fury

But,

By then she had decided

She was nothing without him.

(He got in the way of

every conversation,

every dream of a journey

every blank canvas.)

He'd warned her, and she'd known it,

He'd hurt her.

Until,

Her bones became one of his secrets.

Swimming in an Ocean

Ashley Lambright

Slipping, slipping, slide away.
Where I'm going I don't know.
I'm vulnerable, it's plain to see,
Yet I cannot let it show.

Reassembled delicately,
My fractured soul is leery.
Ready to run and ready to fight,
The rest of me is weary

The mask I wield is hard and cold
To hide my true emotion.
To be myself and risk the pain
Is like swimming in an ocean.

I fear my heart no longer works,
Nor understands its function.
Options to weigh, a choice to make,
For I'm standing at a junction.

Afraid to feel, afraid to fall,
Or to be made of stone.
Afraid that I will lose it all,
Or find that I'm alone.

You terrify and petrify,
When you comfort and you hold.

I withdraw, refuse, rebel
Then I crumble and I fold.

I seek your face when I need a friend,
Someone to make me smile
I completely leave it up to you
To go the extra mile

The question now, to make my point,
Is do I let fear win.
Close the door and shut you out,
Or do I let you in

Recitation Island

Jo Barbara Taylor

lies three buoys and a trawler
off the main coast, its outline
like a ballpoint pen
pointed east to write
a poem on the horizon

a poem of daybreak
and eventide, of seabird wings
to rhyme the way, the glint
of iambic waves
to meter the journey

and in what port, what light
will the journey end
verse jammed next to verse
like rusty ships
no longer able to make a voyage

in the gleam of their heyday
they carried lilting words
and glowing lines, polished titles
each an island
reciting its verse

Citrus

Vonnie Winslow Crist

At the seashore,
in a rented room,
a tangerine sun speared
by the blue atlas cedar dribbles
light through our open window.

Sunshine puddles in sheet gullies,
washes across the bed,
spills onto the wooden floor.

My nostrils quiver
at the salty scent of ocean
as my fingertips stroke
your rough-as-lemon-skin cheeks.

I laugh at the gulls calling
for us to join them on the beach,
then kiss stray droplets
of daylight from your lips.

Ah, morning,
morning is orange—
our blankets are awash

A Burning Love

Joanne Alfano

Yesterday's fire disappears but for ashes;
cinders dust my world;
windowpanes bleed rain and ribbon droplets.
Daylight takes the sun for granted,
while cold fingers seek warmth

Even after burning, there are remains:
newspapers, cigarette wrappers and cereal boxes all
shrivel and die. Except hope –
all that has burned
has left its testament in ashes.

Wednesday I am coated gray in dust
Thursday I eat and drink, sup in grace
Friday, a cruel necessary death
Saturday, no thing, me or any thing
Sunday by tradition or habit, I rise again
lift a match to a crown of logs and wait again
and burn again for Wednesday.

Once when I dared April to challenge
December in my mind's battlefield
the duel raged with swords flaming.
(April had no second, so the fool showed up)
The fire pierced December
in shafts of molten iron spilling the sun
and left no ashes.

My body peels off its acrylic bark
and allows hope to ravish me.
The flames tickle my skin and terrify me.
Not burning, I am consumed;
not ashes, I am whole
strong green fresh new young
when you love me.

Ocean

Leela Soma

Listen, listen to the ocean, it's poetry without words
the waves rising and crashing, the tiny waves with
bubbling foam gurgling gently, brushing the golden
sand, washed pristine again. Musical rivulets on pebbles
a song, cresting over shells and crabs. Tide recedes slowly.

Listen, listen to the rhythm, nature's song for you
hold the conch to your ear, and relive your origin.
Life began with music, listen, listen to the subconscious
the strings of sound that made you a sentient being.
Listen, listen as you sit in silence on the shore.

The Mermaid & The Mariner

Sylvia Riojas Vaughn

On a rolling deck, memories
of a sea dwelling nymph.
Upon their parting in the South Seas,
they exchanged coral keepsakes.
His dangles round his sun kissed neck.
All day he dreams of her
chestnut mane, warm salty lips.
Through the Suez, Panama canals,
crossing the equator over and over,
savoring spices from foreign lands,
he hungers to caress her smooth skin.
On a wharf, he sips coffee, scans
the horizon, listens for her song.
His fervent gaze shifts to the surf.
Maybe she'll appear, shaky on new legs,
joyous gulls wheeling overhead.

The Separation

Laurie Kolp

With leaden legs we cycle
  through seditious seas, count fins we see
  slicing waves, fins
      in different patterns: flounder, catfish, even
shark
  fins too close for comfort, yet
conforming   each species   facetious
  through this deluge
      trying.to.stay.together.
  My achy arms
      draw figure eights
  as I struggle here with you—
just last week
  we watched the western sun
      kiss crystal.

Starlight

Sara Mosier

we are entwined
       in the golden ribbons
              of
                     light
that disturb the
       night-sky water
as it laps memories
away from the lips
of the storm-weary
            shore
and here we stand
       damp eyed
       and
            breathless
as the diamond-like sand rises up
       clinging to our lashes

In Heaven

Jensen Reed

For Ma
V3

I'll see you up in heaven,
Where the yellow roses sway,
On the sea's endless beaches,
Where our horses run and play.

I'll see you up in heaven,
I'll get to hear your laugh.
You'll smile again and show me
That your pain was in the past.

I'll see you up in heaven,
And we'll walk side by side.
Talk about the lives we had,
And chase the changing tide.

I'll see you up in heaven,

Where the rainbow bridge starts.
We will bask in all their love,
While making up for time apart.

I'll see you up in heaven,
Where the years won't seem so long.
I won't be brought to tears,
When I hear your favorite song.

I'll see you up in heaven.
But for now I must stay here.
Though I miss you dearly,
I know you're always there.

Conditions

Katrina Thornley

Caress my words

The way you do my hips,

Kiss the thoughts

Deeper than my lips

And then maybe

We'll find a love worth chasing.

Echoes of Yesteryears

Gabriella Balcom

Laughing, glowing child.
Chubby cheeks, velvety skin.
Golden hair, dark blue eyes.
A dimple in your chin.

Giggles floating in the air.
Watching eyes adoring be.
Twirling body, racing feet.
Arms thrown around me.

Memories day after day.
Happiness, laughter, tears.
Always I hear echoes
Of all the yesteryears.

Wave

Haley Morgan McKinnon

a human body is made
of the same ratio of salt to water
as the sea

I have always assumed that I was
filled with ocean,
that if you sliced me open I would pour out
in waves that reflect the sky,
my skin turned to sand by
the storms inside their hands
my sea-glass bones too beautiful
to leave behind

lay your head against my chest, my love,
may the rhythmic break of swells within my heart
rock you to sleep

Wildfire

Ariella Vasquez

One glance.
That's all it takes
for my heart to ignite the flame.
It spreads like wildfire.

The greenest of trees painted
redder than your soft lips.
Even as I crumble to ash,
I still lust
for those vibrant flames.

Take Me to the Sea

Maxine Churchman

Oh, take me to the sea today,
To see the boats and hear the gulls,
To walk upon the golden sands
And frolic in the spray.

I want to stroll along the prom
To feel the sun upon my face,
To nod at people as they pass
And wonder where they're from.

Oh, take me to the sea, I plead
To sit on benches warm and smooth,
To watch the gulls swoop down for chips
And marvel at their greed.

I want to run along the pier
To see the sea beneath the boards,
To dream of pirates setting sail

And feel a thrill of fear.

Oh, take me to the sea, Dad, please
We'll breathe clean air and rest our legs
In stripy deckchairs on the beach
Then come home for our teas.

This is a Place

Johann Van Der Walt

lost in my thoughts I yield along the arc of a long crescent beach
where I notice an old woman with grey hair in a blue windbreaker
submerged waist deep into the rushed oncoming change of tide
quivering bony hands tightly grip a lengthy deep-sea fishing rod

hidden in plain view is far more to this moment than one simply *sees,*
she stands woman alone defiantly equipped to conquer the impatient sea
 saltwater has become so sweet she doesn't know anything else
except for hours spent contemplating life as a fish, dancing in the surf

the fluidity and precision of well-timed tasks speaks loud about methods
acquiring dinner lies behind her fight against the shadows of sunset
similar to the daily mêlée her body wages against time that slips away,
then a tug and bite declares a sweet victory and tonight she will feast

I sit and wallow under the weight of this moment as life passes me by
woefully staring as she returns to face the swell - the fish was too small -
she deliberates conservancy even when the release prolongs her mission

168

struggling for sustenance — the arduous outcome wasn't chosen in vain -

in that moment I realized that everything will eventually come to this:
we live between the waves of introspection and currents of difficult
decisions
the shallows are often stormier than the open sea, but no shortcut ever led
anyone to a place where they simply became honest human beings
miraculously

it doesn't matter who you are, sink or swim
virtue is a place that already exists within

Southern Comfort

Tyson West

Sinews of sweet take shape
In our Piedmont August night as I enfiladed
Blue-green bronze confederate heroes
Guarding humid streets, to arrive
Naked on Charlotte's bed at the top floor
Of the crumbling Fan District brick three story walk up.
Sheets sweat-soaked
Bourbon fumes decanted in our whispers
Her red painted toes caress my moon pale thigh
Smoke from our cigarettes entwines then
Dances visible in shafts of moonlight
We lie certain that save
For the little death we just endured
We were bound to never die.

February, 2019

Crashing

Laurie Kolp

The roll of your tongue on my sunburned skin
       molds me into you and makes a salty
massage on edge, a stinging fin.
       The roll of your tongue on my sunburned skin
breaks waves, dashes grit against my shin
       rising up, your kiss the brackish sea.
The roll of your tongue on my sunburned skin
       molds me into you and makes me salty.

Whispers

Joanne Alfano

Sparkling eyes and white straight teeth
flashed at me in the dark
and I felt his strong arm
tunnel under my neck and around my shoulders.
In the dark we are legs and arms knitted together
like yarn after cat's play.
It had been a long night
(whispers, sex, moans, secrets)
and now we are spent,
lost in a rumple of sheets and tossed bedclothes
searching for the spot we found in each other
last night in the dark
The spot where we forgot loneliness
and knew vulnerability.
the spot where the walls tumbled
and the future seemed as vast as a western sunset.
We are lost now in the light
what was whispered last night is not forgotten,
merely lost in morning noise:
> the buzz of the alarm
> the toilet flushing
> the hum of an electric toothbrush
> the blare of morning news
all victors in the battle over intimacy.

The Last Returning Tides of Love

Mark Andrew Heathcote

Let's sigh at the quietude of the moon
And know a lover resides at her loom.

Ah, breasts rising high and then falling low,
Pale her dark hair dreams of her Romeo.

Her heart twists in its harsh, tight binding cords
Like a lost cormorant swimming seawards.

With a noose, a twine tied around her neck
She swallows entire oceans bottleneck.

To drink of last returning ebbs of love
Tell of an island the soul-can but dove.

Let's sigh at the quietude of the moon
And know a lover lies sleeping entomb.

Dreaming, miracles that awake the dead
With kisses that wake the soul newlywed.

For more information about the authors featured in this anthology, please visit:

www.stormyislandpublishing.com/publications/sea-glass-hearts

Made in the USA
Lexington, KY
04 November 2019

56558226R00112